TO THE STUDENT:

In this workbook you will learn how Americans communicate in handwritten form.

Here are some helpful rules to remember:

1. Use a pencil with a good eraser.

2. Clear away other books and papers when you write.

3. Don't squeeze the pencil! Your fingers will hurt.

4. Sit up straight and keep your writing arm on the desk or table.

5. The letters of American English are written in a left to right motion.

6. The words and sentences are also written from left to right.

7. Leave a space between each word.

8. Some letters extend below the line.

9. Capital letters are bigger.

10. Write your signature in cursive letters.

Good luck to you! I know you will do a good job.

Janette M. Haynes
Maryland, U.S.A.

TEACHERS, ASSISTANTS AND TUTORS:

This workbook presents American handwriting in both printed and cursive forms. The standard used is everyday script that is legible to literate people in this society. This book has been used successfully by students from every part of the world. It is intended for use as a text for the writing portion of ESL workplace or classroom instruction. As such, it lays the foundation for reading. It works well with adolescents as well as adult students. This book is especially effective in multilevel classes.

Students who benefit most from this workbook fall into three main groups:

1. Those who are unfamiliar with roman letters.

   This student comes from North Africa, the Middle East, Eastern Europe or Asia and did not study English there.

2. Those who did not learn to write in their native language.

   This student can come from anywhere in the world.

3. Those who wish to improve their handwriting skills.

   This student can come from anywhere in the world.

GOALS:

Upon successful completion of this workbook, the student can:

- Sign his/her name in legible script
- Fill in blanks and boxes in both printed and cursive lettering
- Address an envelope
- Write a check or money order
- Write time and money expressions
- Express dates in numbers
- Read and fill out basic forms, including:

     Personal Data Form
     Application for Library Card
     Send a package
     Party Invitation
     Telephone Message
     Money Order

J.M.H.

METHOD AND HELPFUL HINTS FOR INSTRUCTORS

Provide an uncluttered and quiet place for handwriting. Help students to hold the pencil correctly in the dominant hand. Students who are new to writing sometimes hold the pencil so tightly that their fingers hurt after a few minutes. Watch for this. Encourage them to sit up straight with the writing arm resting on the writing table or desk. Beginning writers like to do a good job and do not like to be hurried. Please give them enough time on each page. Students will write at varying speeds. After about 15 minutes students should shift to another activity.

Pages 1–11   Capital letters are presented in printed and cursive forms. Take care that each student writes the letter in a left to right motion. On page 9 and 10 students must write the alphabet in sequence. Page 11 can be used to show them acceptable alternate forms of any letters or to practice any letters that pose particular problems.

Pages 12–19   The lower case letters are presented in printed and cursive forms. Take care that each letter is written in a left to right motion. Watch for these common mistakes:
        Many students will have trouble with the letters that extend below the line.
        Some will make the small "s" so big that it looks like a capital "S."
        The shaded area helps them to size all the lower case letters.
        The "q" is often confused with "g."

Pages 20–22   Further practice on those letters that extend below the line. Most students who do not know the Roman alphabet will need this extra practice.

Page 23   Shows the alternate (quite common) cursive "r," "k," and "t"—letters frequently requiring extra practice.

Pages 24–25   Students practice the lower case alphabet in sequence.

Page 26   The alphabet in capital and lower case letters in both printed and cursive forms.

Page 27   Practice the more difficult letters.

Pages 28–35   Students learn to connect letters by writing out the names of the fifty states of the United States, postal abbreviations, Washington, DC and some of the most populous cities. On page 35 there is room to practice writing the name of the city and the state or territory where the student resides. Help students label the map on page 96.

Pages 36–39   Page 36 teaches the student to fill in a box form. Many do not leave a space between parts of their names. The teacher must help them understand what is meant by "first name," "last name," "middle name," and "middle initial." On page 37 the students fill in the boxes with their own names. Note that they are asked to print. On page 38 they must both print and write their names. By page 39 students should understand what is meant by *Signature: Print your name:* and *Sign your name:*

Pages 40–51   Numbers are written out in numerals and words in both printed and cursive forms. Help students place the hyphen correctly above the line. Ordinals are also used. There are practice pages included.

Pages 52–53   Use these pages to practice any problem numbers and correct placement of the hyphen.

Pages 54–56   Teaches students how we express money in numbers and words.

Page 57   Many students do not realize that Americans use two dots (:) for time expressions and one dot (.) (i.e., the decimal point) for money.

Pages 58–61	Teaches the usual American style of writing a check. Be sure that they sign a legible signature on the practice checks.
Pages 62–65	Days, months and common abbreviations. Show the students how numbers correspond to months.
Pages 66–67	Presents common abbreviations for streets. Help your students learn their own street names and abbreviations. Add others to the bottom of the page if needed.
Page 68	Helps students to distinguish between Zip Code and Area Code.
Pages 69–71	Students need help to learn the different elements of "Address." Tell them that "Number" means "House Number" or "Building Number." Also that "Apartment Number" is always entered after the name of the street or on the right side of the envelope.
Pages 72–73	Americans usually express dates in this order: Month–Day–Year. Students do need to practice this order.
Page 74	Students need to learn their Social Security Number and how to enter it in several different forms.
Page 75	Practice writing several sentences. Help them to place a period at the end of a sentence.
Page 76	Students fill in the Personal Data Form. Teachers may substitute another number in place of "Driver's License Number." (Alien Registration Number, Passport Number, Student Identification Number, etc.)
Page 77	Titles should be explained. Help them to check the correct box and circle the correct title.
Pages 78–80	Students fill out the forms. Here they will use the information learned in the preceding pages. Note that students are instructed, "DO NOT WRITE BELOW THIS LINE" on page 80. Explain that they do not write any information beneath the broken line.
Page 81	Students may work with a partner. They should enter information on the form sending a sweater to the partner.
Page 82	Students fill in a typical party invitation form using their own names, addresses and telephone numbers. Remember: RSVP means "Please respond."
Pages 83–84	Students copy information onto simple telephone message forms. On page 84 be sure that students sign their own names to the message.
Pages 85–86	Money Order. Check to see that the address was entered correctly. Students may work with partners.
Pages 87–95	These pages allow students to practice writing personal data in spaces of narrower width.
Page 96	Students should label this map when working on pages 28–35.

American Handwriting

AMERICAN HANDWRITING
Slow and Easy
TABLE OF CONTENTS

THE ALPHABET
CAPITAL LETTERS

A B C D E F G H I

J K L M N O P Q R

S T U V W X Y Z

A B C D E F G H I

J K L M N O P Q R

S T U V W X Y Z

CAPITAL LETTERS

COPY: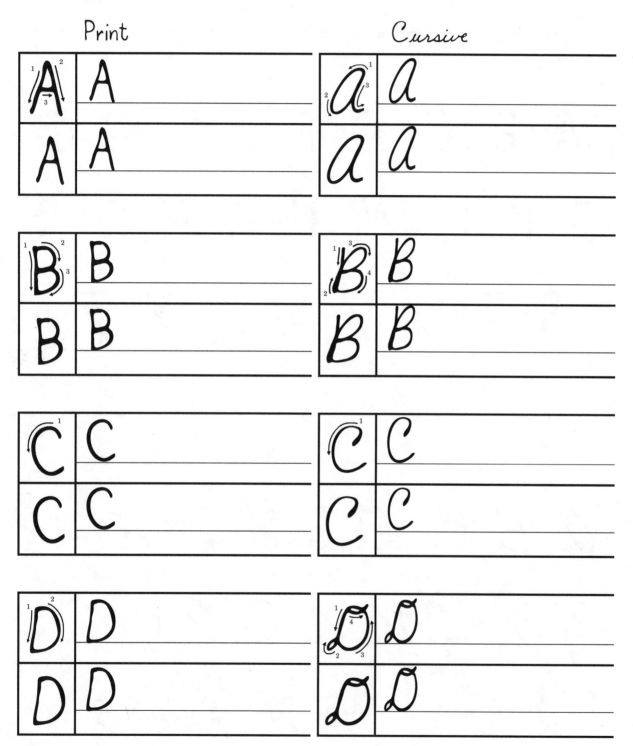

Print

Cursive

CAPITAL LETTERS

COPY: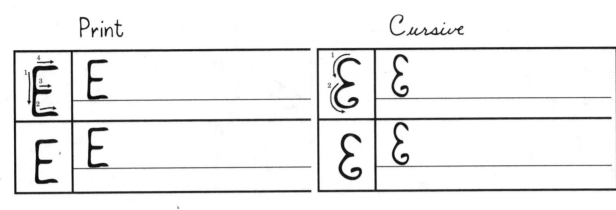

Print   Cursive

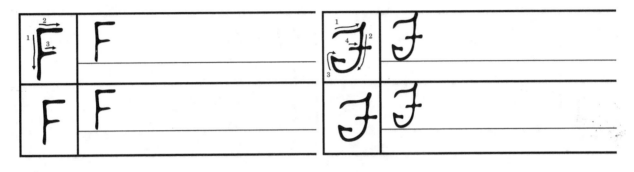

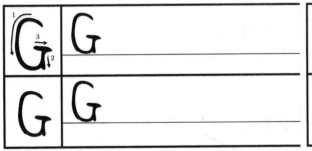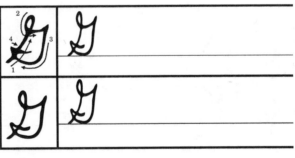

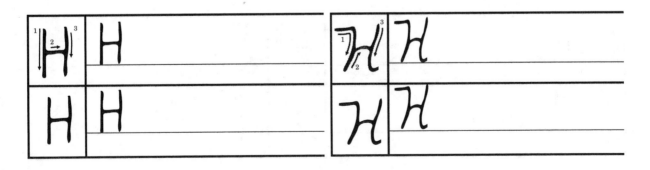

CAPITAL LETTERS

COPY:

Print   Cursive

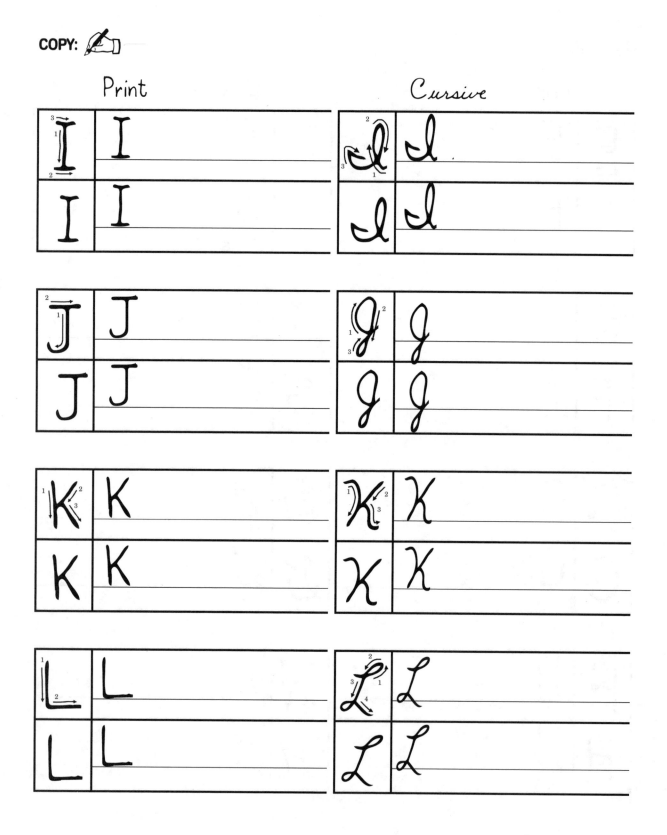

CAPITAL LETTERS

COPY: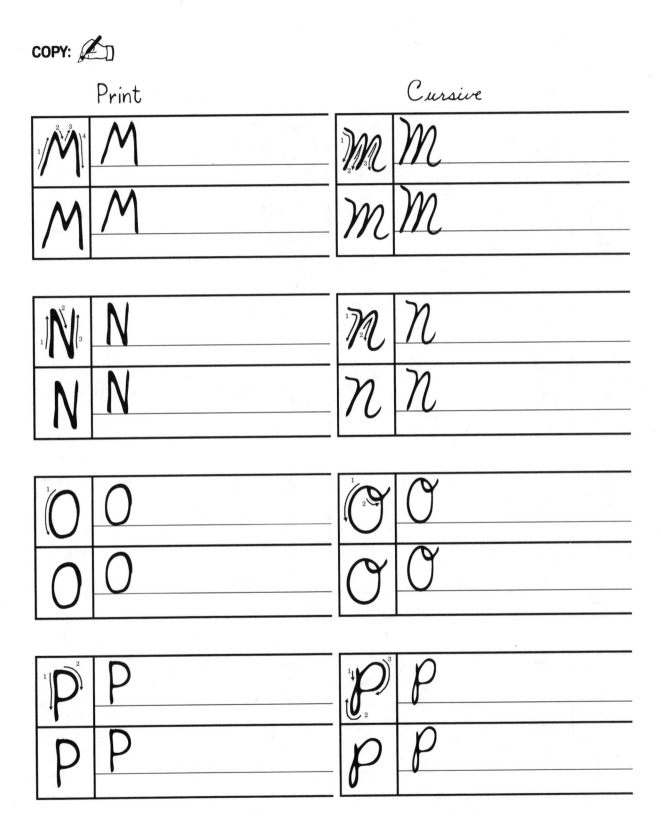

Print   Cursive

CAPITAL LETTERS

COPY:

Print   Cursive

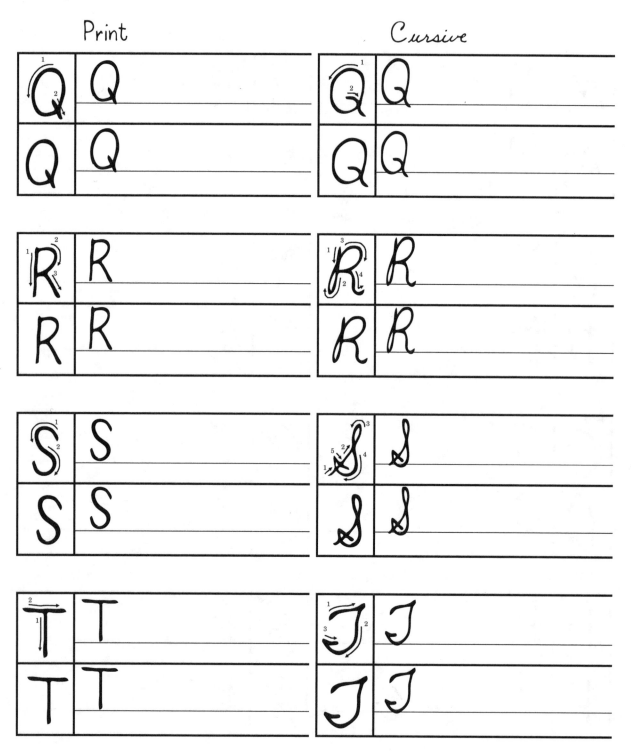

American Handwriting

CAPITAL LETTERS

COPY:

Print   Cursive

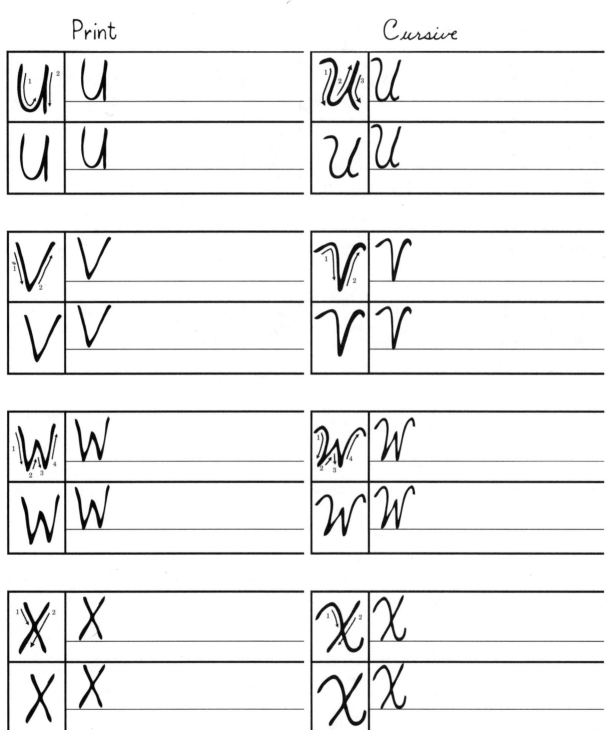

CAPITAL LETTERS

Print

Cursive

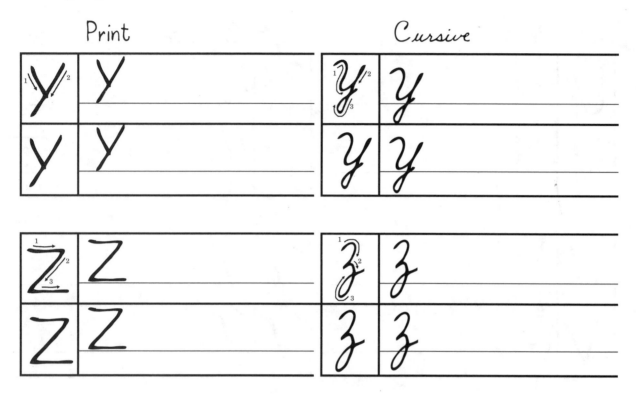

Print	Cursive
A	$\mathcal{A}$
B	$\mathcal{B}$
C	$\mathcal{C}$
D	$\mathcal{D}$
E	$\mathcal{E}$
F	$\mathcal{F}$
G	$\mathcal{G}$
H	$\mathcal{H}$
I	$\mathcal{I}$
J	$\mathcal{J}$
K	$\mathcal{K}$
L	$\mathcal{L}$
M	$\mathcal{m}$
N	$\mathcal{n}$
O	$\mathcal{O}$
P	$\mathcal{P}$
Q	$\mathcal{Q}$
R	$\mathcal{R}$
S	$\mathcal{S}$
T	$\mathcal{T}$
U	$\mathcal{U}$
V	$\mathcal{V}$
W	$\mathcal{W}$
X	$\mathcal{X}$
Y	$\mathcal{Y}$
Z	$\mathcal{z}$

THE ALPHABET

COPY THE CAPITAL LETTERS:

A B C D E F G H I
J K L M N O P Q R
S T U V W X Y Z

Print the Capital Letters: ↓

_ _ _ _ _ _ _ _

_ _ _ _ _ _ _ _

_ _ _ _ _ _ _ _

A B C D E F G H I
J K L M N O P Q R
S T U V W X Y Z

Write the Capital Letters: ↓

_ _ _ _ _ _ _ _

_ _ _ _ _ _ _ _

_ _ _ _ _ _ _ _

PRACTICE WRITING

D

G   *g*

I

J

P

S

Q

a b c d e f g h i

j k l m n o p q r

s t u v w x y z

a b c d e f g h i

j k l m n o p q r

s t u v w x y z

Lower Case Letters

COPY: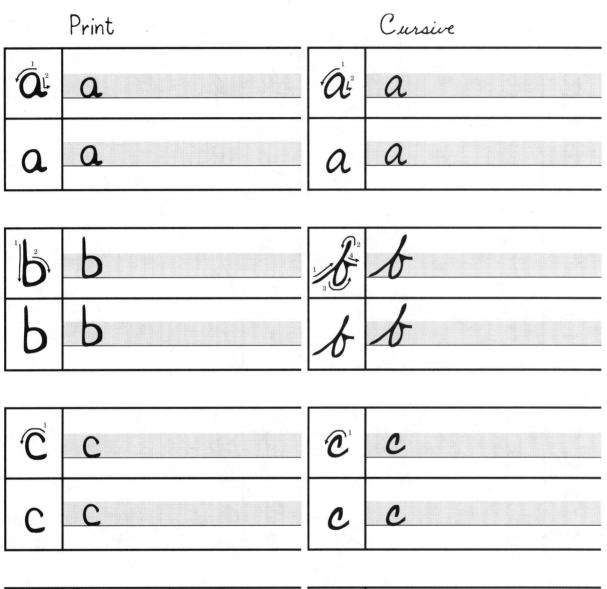

Print

Cursive

Lower Case Letters

COPY:

Print   Cursive

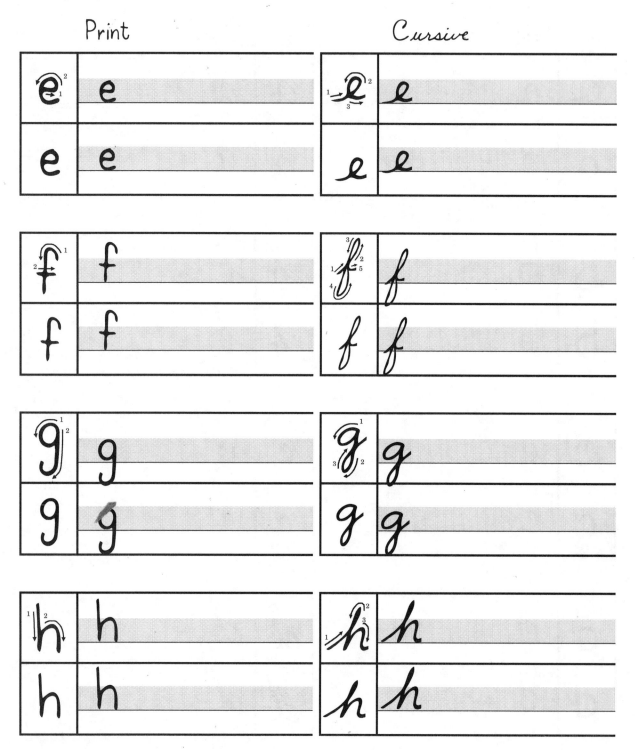

Lower Case Letters

COPY: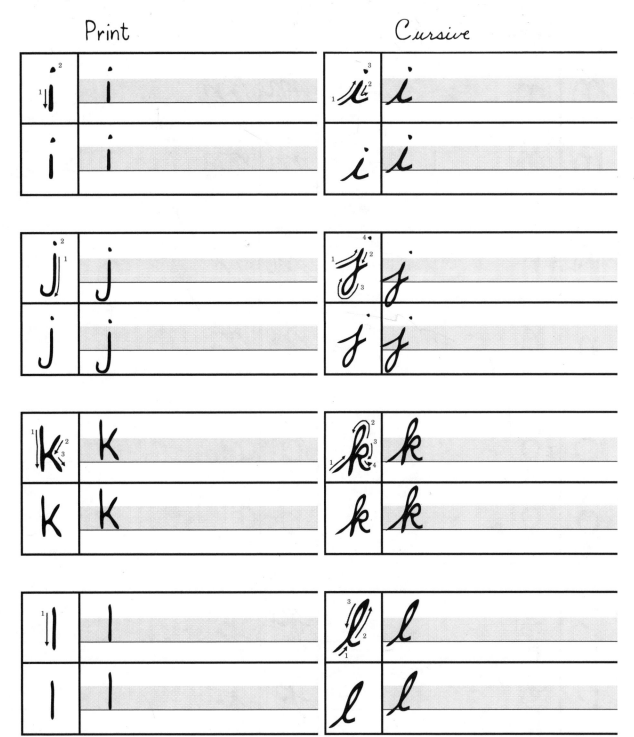

Print   Cursive

Lower Case Letters

Print   Cursive

m   m   m   m

m   m   m   m

n   n   n   n

n   n   n   n

o   o   o   o

o   o   o   o

p   p   p   p

p   p   p   p

Lower Case Letters

COPY: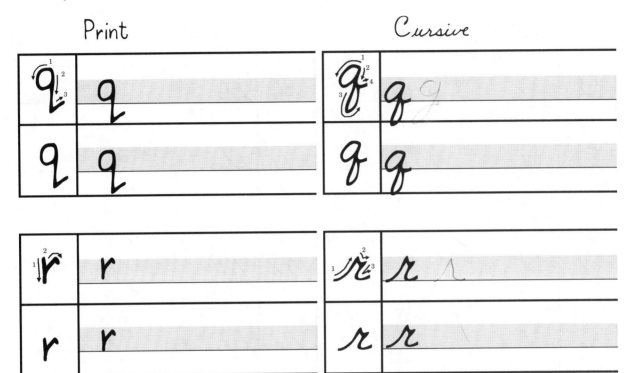

Print   Cursive

q   q   q   q   q

q   q   q   q

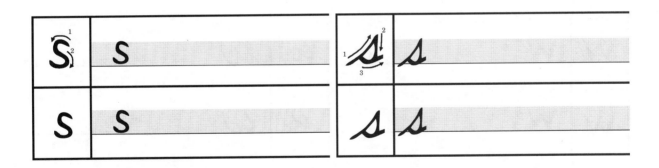

r   r   r   r

r   r   r   r

s   s   s   s

s   s   s   s

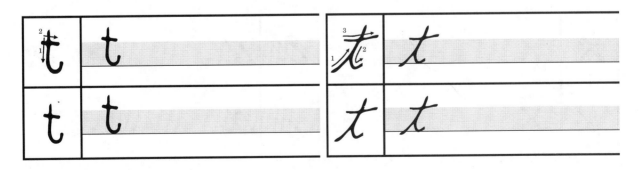

t   t   t   t

t   t   t   t

Lower Case Letters

Print

Cursive

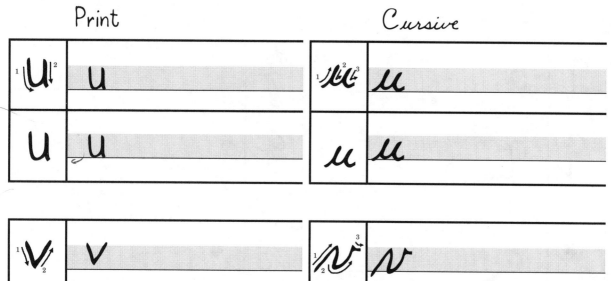

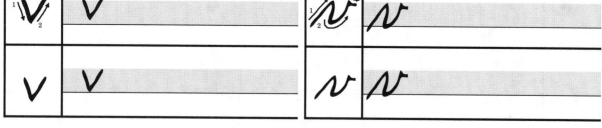

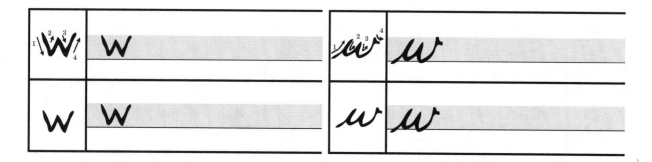

Lower Case Letters

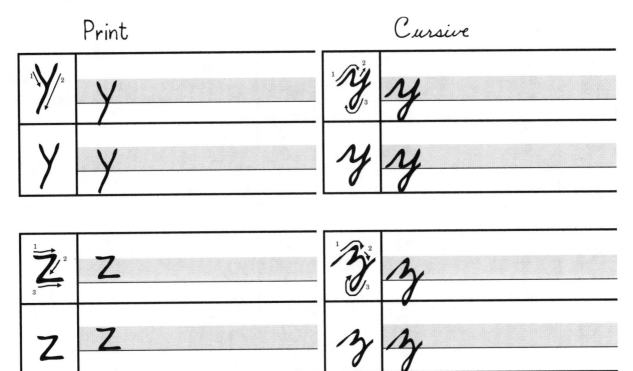

COPY:

Print

Cursive

Problem Lower Case Letters

COPY:

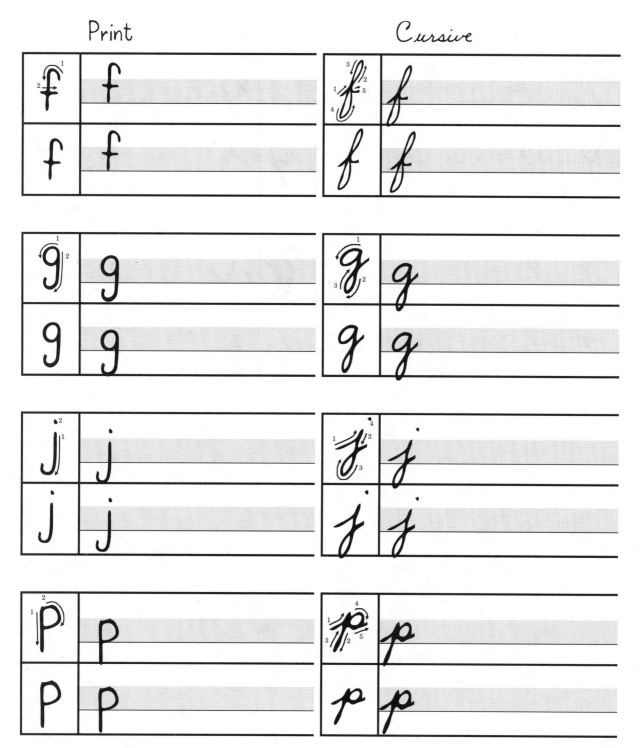

Print

Cursive

American Handwriting

Problem Lower Case Letters

COPY: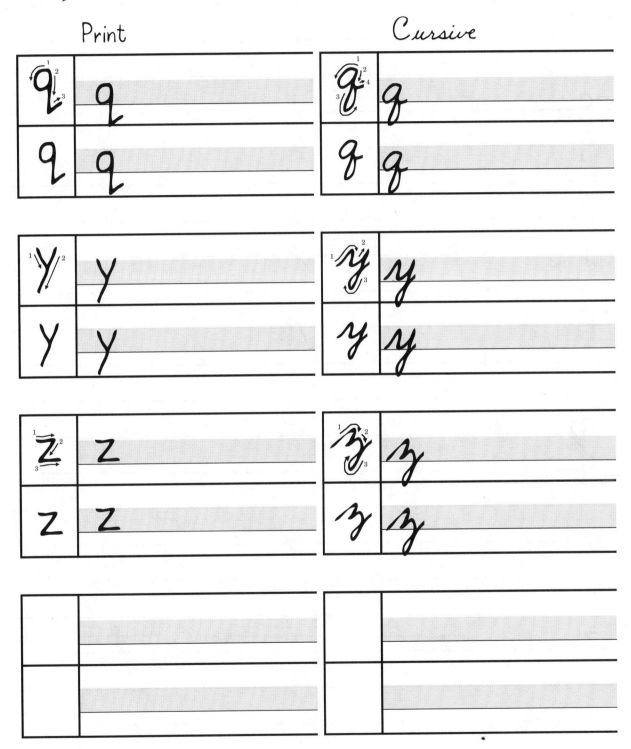

Print   Cursive

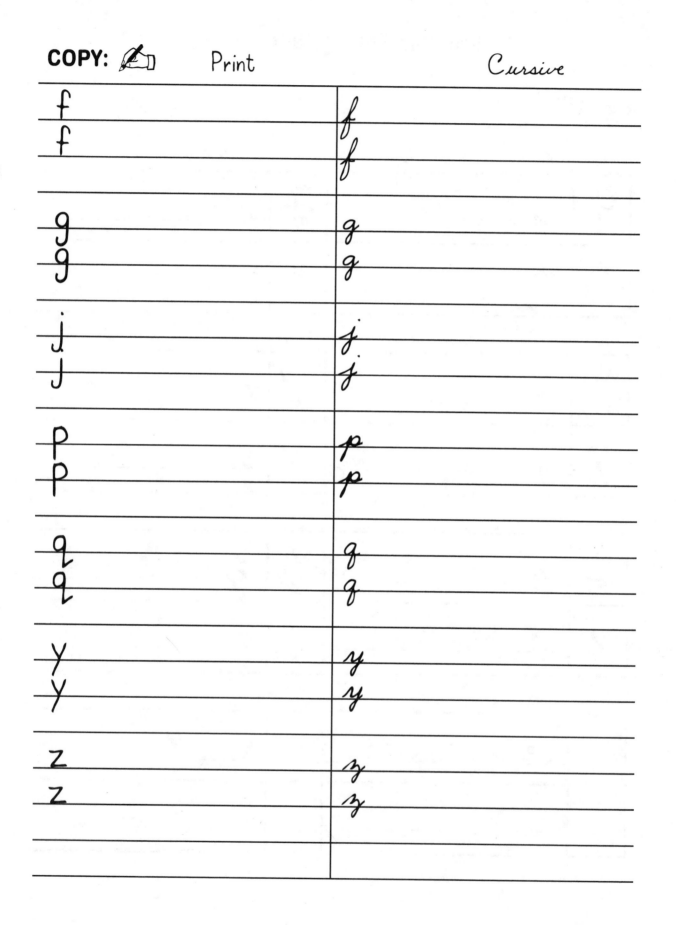

f   f
f   f
                                           f

g   g
g   g

j   j.
j   j

p   p
p   p

q   q
q   q

y   y
y   y

z   z
z   z

Practice Writing

b

d

f

h

n

k   K

p

r   r

x

t   t

Print	Cursive
a	a
b	b
c	c
d	d
e	e
f	f
g	g
h	h
i	i
j	j
k	k
l	l
m	m
n	n
o	o
p	p
q	q
r	r
s	s
t	t
u	u
v	v
w	w
x	x
y	y
z	z

THE ALPHABET

COPY THE LOWER CASE LETTERS:

a b c d e f g h i
j k l m n o p q r
s t u v w x y z

Print the Lower Case Letters: ↓

_ _ _ _ _ _ _ _ _ _ _ _ _

_ _ _ _ _ _ _ _ _ _ _ _ _

_ _ _ _ _ _ _ _ _ _ _ _ _

---

a b c d e f g h i
j k l m n o p q r
s t u v w x y z

Write the Lower Case Letters: ↓

_ _ _ _ _ _ _ _ _ _ _ _ _

_ _ _ _ _ _ _ _ _ _ _ _ _

_ _ _ _ _ _ _ _ _ _ _ _ _

	Print		Cursive
A	a	*A*	*a*
B	b	*B*	*b*
C	c	*C*	*c*
D	d	*D*	*d*
E	e	*E*	*e*
F	f	*F*	*f*
G	g	*G*	*g*
H	h	*H*	*h*
I	i	*I*	*i*
J	j	*J*	*j*
K	k	*K*	*k*
L	l	*L*	*l*
M	m	*M*	*m*
N	n	*N*	*n*
O	o	*O*	*o*
P	p	*P*	*p*
Q	q	*Q*	*q*
R	r	*R*	*r*
S	s	*S*	*s*
T	t	*T*	*t*
U	u	*U*	*u*
V	v	*V*	*v*
W	w	*W*	*w*
X	x	*X*	*x*
Y	y	*Y*	*y*
Z	z	*Z*	*z*

PRACTICE WRITING

UNITED STATES OF AMERICA

COPY:

Abbreviation:	Print	Cursive
AL	Alabama	Alabama
AK	Alaska	Alaska
AZ	Arizona	Arizona
AR	Arkansas	Arkansas
CA	California	California
CO	Colorado	Colorado
CT	Connecticut	Connecticut
DE	Delaware	Delaware
FL	Florida	Florida
GA	Georgia	Georgia

American Handwriting

UNITED STATES OF AMERICA

COPY:

Abbreviation:	Print	Cursive
HI	Hawaii	Hawaii
ID	Idaho	Idaho
IL	Illinois	Illinois
IN	Indiana	Indiana
IA	Iowa	Iowa
KS	Kansas	Kansas
KY	Kentucky	Kentucky
LA	Louisiana	Louisiana
ME	Maine	Maine
MD	Maryland	Maryland

UNITED STATES OF AMERICA

Abbreviation:	Print	Cursive
MA	Massachusetts	Massachusetts
MI	Michigan	Michigan
MN	Minnesota	Minnesota
MS	Mississippi	Mississippi
MO	Missouri	Missouri
MT	Montana	Montana
NE	Nebraska	Nebraska
NV	Nevada	Nevada
NH	New Hampshire	New Hampshire
NJ	New Jersey	New Jersey

UNITED STATES OF AMERICA

COPY:

Abbreviation:	Print	Cursive
NM	New Mexico	New Mexico
NY	New York	New York
NC	North Carolina	North Carolina
ND	North Dakota	North Dakota
OH	Ohio	Ohio
OK	Oklahoma	Oklahoma
OR	Oregon	Oregon
PA	Pennsylvania	Pennsylvania
RI	Rhode Island	Rhode Island
SC	South Carolina	South Carolina

UNITED STATES OF AMERICA

COPY:

Abbreviation:	Print	Cursive
SD	South Dakota	South Dakota
TN	Tennessee	Tennessee
TX	Texas	Texas
UT	Utah	Utah
VT	Vermont	Vermont
VA	Virginia	Virginia
WA	Washington	Washington
WV	West Virginia	West Virginia
WI	Wisconsin	Wisconsin
WY	Wyoming	Wyoming

American Handwriting

UNITED STATES OF AMERICA

COPY:

Capital City

Abbreviation:	Print	Cursive
DC	Washington, DC	Washington, DC

U.S. CITIES

COPY:

Print	Cursive
Los Angeles	Los Angeles
New York	New York
Dallas	Dallas
Miami	Miami
Chicago	Chicago

PRACTICE WRITING

California

Texas

Florida

New York

Arizona

Illinois

Maryland

Virginia

Washington

PRACTICE WRITING

NAME

Example: Charles William Haynes

C	h	a	r	l	e	s		W	i	l	l	i	a	m		H	a	y	n	e	s			

FULL NAME = Charles William Haynes
FIRST NAME = Charles
MIDDLE NAME = William
MIDDLE INITIAL = **M.I.** = W.
LAST NAME = **FAMILY NAME** = Haynes

FILL OUT THE FORM BELOW FOR CHARLES

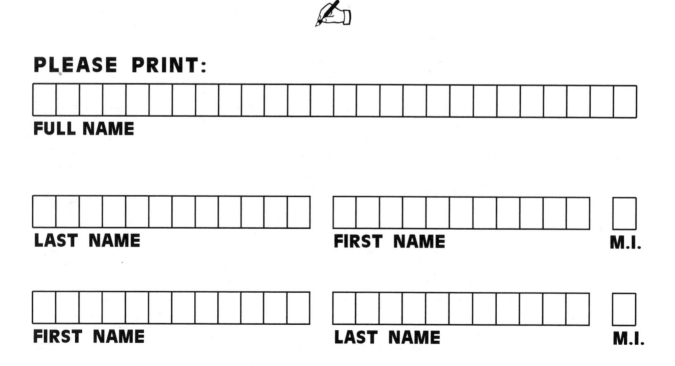

PLEASE PRINT:

FULL NAME

LAST NAME   FIRST NAME   M.I.

FIRST NAME   LAST NAME   M.I.

YOUR NAME

FILL OUT THE FORM

PRINT YOUR FULL NAME

```
☐☐☐☐☐☐☐☐☐☐☐☐☐☐☐☐☐☐☐☐☐☐☐☐☐☐☐☐
```

PLEASE PRINT:

```
☐☐☐☐☐☐☐☐☐☐☐☐☐          ☐☐☐☐☐☐☐☐☐☐☐☐☐      ☐
```
LAST NAME   FIRST NAME   M.I.

```
☐☐☐☐☐☐☐☐☐☐☐☐☐          ☐          ☐☐☐☐☐☐☐☐☐☐☐☐☐
```
FIRST NAME   M.I.   LAST NAME

FILL OUT THE FORM

PRINT PLEASE:

```
☐☐☐☐☐☐☐☐☐☐☐☐☐☐☐☐☐☐☐☐☐☐☐☐☐☐☐☐
```
YOUR FULL NAME

```
☐☐☐☐☐☐☐☐☐☐☐☐☐          ☐☐☐☐☐☐☐☐☐☐☐☐☐      ☐
```
LAST NAME   FIRST NAME   M.I.

```
☐☐☐☐☐☐☐☐☐☐☐☐☐          ☐          ☐☐☐☐☐☐☐☐☐☐☐☐☐
```
FIRST NAME   M.I.   LAST NAME

FIRST NAME   LAST NAME

Print your first name: Print your last name:

1.

2.

3.

4.

5.

Write your first name: *Write* your last name:

1.

2.

3.

4.

5.

NAME AND SIGNATURE

PRINT YOUR NAME:	SIGN YOUR NAME:

NUMBERS

1 2 3 4 5 6 7 8 9 10

COPY: ✏️

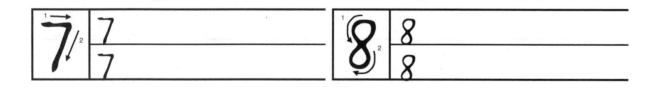

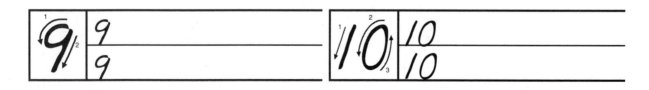

PRACTICE WRITING NUMBERS

NUMBERS

Print   Cursive

Print		Cursive
0	zero	zero
1	one	one
2	two	two
3	three	three
4	four	four
5	five	five
6	six	six
7	seven	seven
8	eight	eight
9	nine	nine
10	ten	ten
11	eleven	eleven

American Handwriting

NUMBERS

12	twelve	*twelve*
13	thirteen	*thirteen*
14	fourteen	*fourteen*
15	fifteen	*fifteen*
16	sixteen	*sixteen*
17	seventeen	*seventeen*
18	eighteen	*eighteen*
19	nineteen	*nineteen*
20	twenty	*twenty*
21	twenty-one	*twenty-one*
22	twenty-two	*twenty-two*
23	twenty-three	*twenty-three*

NUMBERS BY 5's

COPY: ✍   Print   Cursive

	Print	Cursive
5	five	five
10	ten	ten
15	fifteen	fifteen
20	twenty	twenty
25	twenty-five	twenty-five
30	thirty	thirty
35	thirty-five	thirty-five
40	forty	forty
45	forty-five	forty-five
50	fifty	fifty

American Handwriting

NUMBERS BY 5's

COPY:

	Print	Cursive
55	fifty-five	fifty-five
60	sixty	sixty
65	sixty-five	sixty-five
70	seventy	seventy
75	seventy-five	seventy-five
80	eighty	eighty
85	eighty-five	eighty-five
90	ninety	ninety
95	ninety-five	ninety-five
100	one hundred	one hundred

NUMBERS BY 10's

COPY: | Print | Cursive

	Print	Cursive
10	ten	ten
20	twenty	twenty
30	thirty	thirty
40	forty	forty
50	fifty	fifty
60	sixty	sixty
70	seventy	seventy
80	eighty	eighty
90	ninety	ninety
100	one hundred	one hundred

NUMBERS

COPY: ✍ Print

100   one hundred

1,000   one thousand

10,000   ten thousand

100,000   one hundred thousand

1,000,000   one million

COPY: ✍ Cursive

100   one hundred

1,000   one thousand

10,000   ten thousand

100,000   one hundred thousand

1,000,000   one million

American Handwriting   **47**

NUMBERS

COPY: Print   Cursive

	Print	Cursive
21	twenty-one	twenty-one
32	thirty-two	thirty-two
43	forty-three	forty-three
54	fifty-four	fifty-four
65	sixty-five	sixty-five
76	seventy-six	seventy-six
87	eighty-seven	eighty-seven
98	ninety-eight	ninety-eight
109	one hundred nine	one hundred nine

PRACTICE WRITING NUMBERS

ORDINAL NUMBERS

COPY: ✍   Print   Cursive

Print	Cursive
1st first	1st first
2nd second	2nd second
3rd third	3rd third
4th fourth	4th fourth
5th fifth	5th fifth
6th sixth	6th sixth
7th seventh	7th seventh
8th eighth	8th eighth
9th ninth	9th ninth
10th tenth	10th tenth

ORDINAL NUMBERS

COPY: Print   Cursive

Print	Cursive
11th eleventh	11th eleventh
12th twelfth	12th twelfth
13th thirteenth	13th thirteenth
14th fourteenth	14th fourteenth
15th fifteenth	15th fifteenth
20th twentieth	20th twentieth
25th twenty-fifth	25th twenty-fifth
100th one hundredth	100th one hundredth

PRACTICE WRITING NUMBERS

0

1

4

7

9

twenty-seven

forty-two

fifteen

zero

31st

32nd

33rd

34th

35th

PRACTICE WRITING

MONEY

Print	Cursive
money	money
one dollar	one dollar
five dollars	five dollars
ten dollars	ten dollars
twenty dollars	twenty dollars
change	change
coins	coins
bills	bills

MONEY

COPY:

Print	Cursive
penny	penny
pennies	pennies
nickel	nickel
nickels	nickels
dime	dime
dimes	dimes
quarter	quarter
quarters	quarters
coin	coin
coins	coins

DOLLARS AND CENTS

Words	Numbers
one dollar	$1.00
forty-nine cents	$.49 = 49¢
two dollars and one cent	$2.01
eighteen dollars	$18.00
ninety-five cents	$.95 = 95¢

Fill in the numbers:

two dollars	
twenty-nine cents	
six dollars and one cent	
fourteen dollars	
thirty-five cents	

Fill in the words:

	$3.00
	$.59 = 59¢
	$5.01
	$16.00
	$.85 = 85¢
	$7.00

TIME AND MONEY

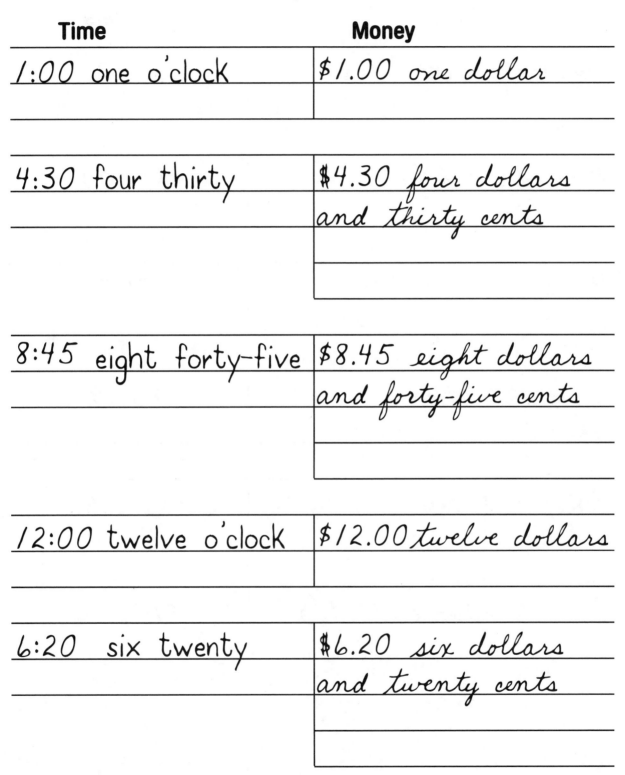

Time	Money
1:00 one o'clock	*$1.00 one dollar*
4:30 four thirty	*$4.30 four dollars and thirty cents*
8:45 eight forty-five	*$8.45 eight dollars and forty-five cents*
12:00 twelve o'clock	*$12.00 twelve dollars*
6:20 six twenty	*$6.20 six dollars and twenty cents*

CHECKS

Words	Numbers
Twenty-four and $^{31}/100$	$24.31
Nineteen and $^{00}/100$	$19.00
Seventy-six and $^{99}/100$	$76.99
Five and $^{29}/100$	$5.29
Sixty-eight and $^{95}/100$	$68.95
One hundred and $^{no}/100$	$100.00

WRITE THE CHECK

TO THE POSTMASTER FOR $100.00

Your Name	
Your Address	Date _7-20-97_

Pay to _____ _Postmaster_ _____ $ _100.00_

One hundred and ⁰⁰/₁₀₀ ⌇⌇⌇ Dollars

THE BANK
BANK ADDRESS

Your Signature

TO THE POSTMASTER FOR $68.95

Your Name	
Your Address	Date _____

Pay to _____ $ _____

_____ Dollars

THE BANK
BANK ADDRESS

_____

WRITE THE CHECK

Practice writing the checks below:

Amount: $89.25

Your Name	
Your Address	Date _____
Pay to _____	$ _____
_____	Dollars
THE BANK	
BANK ADDRESS	_____

Amount: $200.00

Your Name	
Your Address	Date _____
Pay to _____	$ _____
_____	Dollars
THE BANK	
BANK ADDRESS	_____

PRACTICE WRITING

DAYS AND MONTHS

Print	Cursive
Days	Days
Sunday	Sunday
Monday	Monday
Tuesday	Tuesday
Wednesday	Wednesday
Thursday	Thursday
Friday	Friday
Saturday	Saturday
Months	Months
January	January

DAYS AND MONTHS

Print	Cursive
February	February
March	March
April	April
May	May
June	June
July	July
August	August
September	September
October	October
November	November
December	December

DAYS AND MONTHS
Abbreviations

COPY:

Print	Cursive
Sun.	Sun.
Mon.	Mon.
Tues.	Tues.
Wed.	Wed.
Thurs.	Thurs.
Fri.	Fri.
Sat.	Sat.

1 = Jan.	Jan.
2 = Feb.	Feb.
3 = Mar.	Mar.
4 = Apr.	Apr.
5 = May	May
6 = June	June

DAYS AND MONTHS
Abbreviations

Print	Cursive
7 = July	July
8 = Aug.	Aug.
9 = Sept.	Sept.
10 = Oct.	Oct.
11 = Nov.	Nov.
12 = Dec.	Dec.

STREET

COPY:

Abbreviation	Print	Cursive
St.	Street	Street
Ave.	Avenue	Avenue
Blvd.	Boulevard	Boulevard
Rd.	Road	Road
Dr.	Drive	Drive
Hwy.	Highway	Highway
Pkwy.	Parkway	Parkway
Way	Way	Way
Ct.	Court	Court
Ln.	Lane	Lane

STREET

COPY:

Abbreviation | Print | Cursive

Abbreviation	Print	Cursive
Pl.	Place	Place
Terr.	Terrace	Terrace
Cir.	Circle	Circle
Pike	Pike	Pike
Tr.	Trail	Trail
Sq.	Square	Square
Rt.	Route	Route

NUMBERS

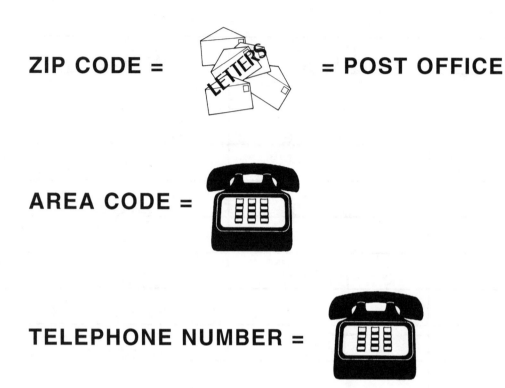

ZIP CODE =   = POST OFFICE

AREA CODE =

TELEPHONE NUMBER =

Fill in your:

Area Code	Telephone Number	Zip Code
( )	—	
( )	—	
( )	—	
( )	—	
( )	—	

ADDRESS

Please print your:

HOUSE NUMBER	STREET	APARTMENT NUMBER

CITY	STATE	ZIP CODE

NAME ADDRESS TELEPHONE

Fill in the boxes. Please print.

MONTH   DAY   YEAR

LAST NAME

FIRST NAME

MI

NUMBER   STREET

APARTMENT

CITY

STATE   ZIP CODE

AREA CODE   TELEPHONE NUMBER

X _____
SIGNATURE

FILL IN THE FORM BELOW

PRINT PLEASE:

MONTH   DAY   YEAR

FIRST NAME

MI   LAST NAME

NUMBER   STREET

APARTMENT

CITY

STATE   ZIP CODE

AREA CODE   TELEPHONE NUMBER

SIGN HERE: X _____

ADDRESS THE ENVELOPE

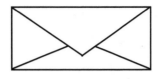

Your name and address: ▼

Address the envelope to a friend: ▼

Return Address =
Your name and address: ▼

Your friend's name and address: ▼

WRITE THE DATES

Example:

    5/30/75   *May 30, 1975* _____

a.   5/09/98   _____

b.   2/26/81   _____

c.   4/5/90   _____

d. 01/22/76   _____

e.   12/3/85   _____

f.   9/19/00   _____

g. 11/30/71   _____

h.   3/14/88   _____

i.   7/01/95   _____

j. 10/07/25   _____

k.   8/15/52   _____

l.   6/08/06   _____

m.   2/3/01   _____

BIRTH DATE

Example:

FEBRUARY 13, 1970 = 2/13/70 = 02–13–70

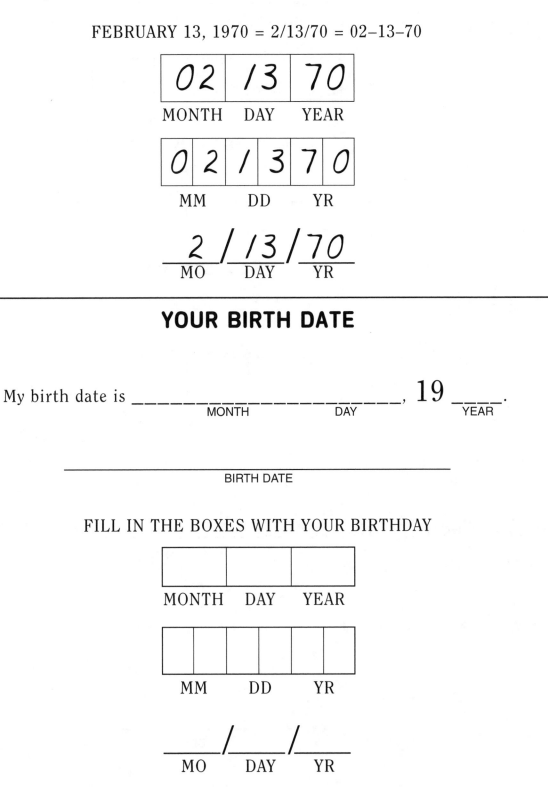

02	13	70
MONTH	DAY	YEAR

0	2	1	3	7	0
MM		DD		YR	

$\underline{2}$ / $\underline{13}$ / $\underline{70}$
MO   DAY   YR

YOUR BIRTH DATE

My birth date is _____, 19 ____.
             MONTH   DAY   YEAR

_____
BIRTH DATE

FILL IN THE BOXES WITH YOUR BIRTHDAY

MONTH	DAY	YEAR

MM		DD		YR

____ / ____ / ____
MO   DAY   YR

SOCIAL SECURITY NUMBER

Fill in your Social Security Number:

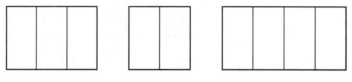

Social Security Number

Soc. Sec. No.

SOCIAL SECURITY NUMBER

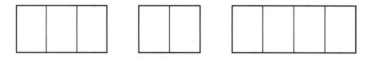

Social Security Number __ __ __ – __ __ – __ __ __ __

Enter your Social Security Number here: _____

SOC. SEC. #

American Handwriting

PRACTICE WRITING

My first name is

My last name is

My phone number is

My birthday is

My address is

PERSONAL DATA

FIRST NAME	SOCIAL SECURITY NUMBER	DATE OF BIRTH

LAST NAME	DRIVER'S LICENSE NUMBER	BIRTH DATE

FIRST NAME	LAST NAME	M.I.	TELEPHONE NUMBER
			( )
			( )
			( )
			( )
			( )

TITLES
MR. MRS. MS. MISS

MR. = MAN

MS. = WOMAN

MRS. = MARRIED WOMAN

MISS = GIRL

SEX
MALE = MAN or BOY

FEMALE = WOMAN or GIRL

CHECK THE BOX

MR. ☐

MS. ☐

MRS. ☐

MISS ☐

MALE = M = Man = ☐

FEMALE = F = Woman = ☐

Example:
Circle: (Mr.)   Ms.   Mrs.   Miss

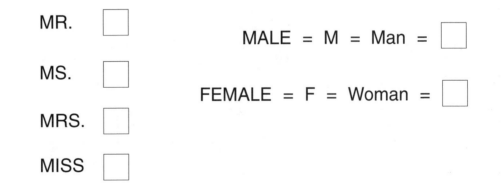

YOU			
Circle one: Mr.	Ms.	Mrs.	Miss
Check (✔)		Check one:	
M ☐		MALE ☐	
F ☐		FEMALE ☐	

PERSONAL DATA

Complete the form. (Please print.)

1. (circle one)   MS.   MRS.   MR.   MISS

2.   Name   _____
             Last   First   Middle Initial

3.   Address _____
             Number   Street   Apt. #

4.   _____
             City   State   ZIP

5.   Sex: Male ☐   Female ☐

6.   Social Security Number   ☐☐☐ – ☐☐ – ☐☐☐☐

7.   Telephone Number   (_____) _____

8.   Birth Date   _____

9.   Driver's License # _____   State _____

10.   ✗ _____   _____
             Signature   Date

APPLICATION

PLEASE PRINT

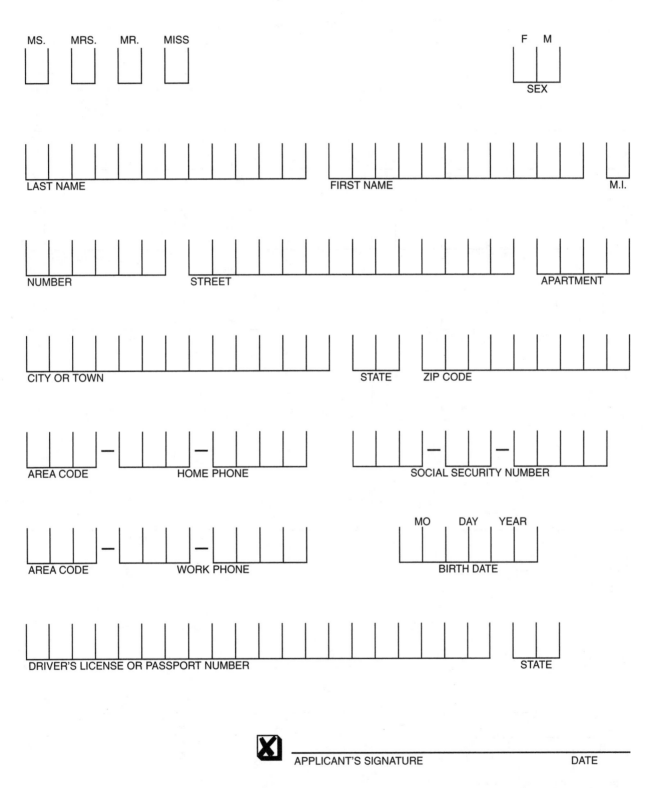

MS.　MRS.　MR.　MISS

F　M

SEX

LAST NAME　　FIRST NAME　　M.I.

NUMBER　　STREET　　APARTMENT

CITY OR TOWN　　STATE　ZIP CODE

AREA CODE　HOME PHONE　　SOCIAL SECURITY NUMBER

AREA CODE　WORK PHONE

MO　DAY　YEAR
BIRTH DATE

DRIVER'S LICENSE OR PASSPORT NUMBER　　STATE

APPLICANT'S SIGNATURE　　DATE

American Handwriting

LIBRARY CARD

DEPARTMENT OF PUBLIC LIBRARIES

REGISTRATION FORM

DATE

LAST NAME   FIRST NAME   MI

NUMBER   STREET   APARTMENT

CITY   STATE   ZIP CODE

TELEPHONE   DRIVER'S LICENSE   BIRTH YEAR

DO NOT WRITE BELOW THIS LINE
===

PLANNING AREA _____   AFFIX LABEL HERE

BORROWER TYPE

SEND A PACKAGE

Send a sweater to a friend:

Customer =   you
Send to   =   your friend
Contents =   sweater

Charge   = $6.45
Tax   =   .25
Total Charges = $6.70

FILL OUT THE FORM:

DATE:	
CUSTOMER: (Please Print)	**SEND TO: (Please Print)**
NAME	NAME
STREET ADDRESS	STREET ADDRESS
CITY/STATE/ZIP	CITY/STATE/ZIP
DAYTIME PHONE	DAYTIME PHONE

CONTENTS:

	CHARGE	
	TAX	
	TOTAL CHARGES	

CUSTOMER'S SIGNATURE:

INVITATION

INVITATION TO A PARTY

Invite a friend to a New Year's Eve party!

When	=	December 31
Time	=	9:00PM
Where	=	your address
Occasion	=	New Year's Eve celebration
RSVP	=	your name and telephone number

Fill in the party invitation:

COME TO A PARTY!

WHEN:

TIME:

WHERE:

OCCASION:

RSVP:

COPY THE MESSAGE

To: Bob

April 22   3:00 PM

Call me at (202) 933-8783.

                    From: Carl

↓

To: _____

Date: _____ Time: _____ AM/PM

MESSAGE

FROM: _____

TELEPHONE MESSAGE

IMPORTANT MESSAGE
URGENT ☐

TO _____

DATE _____ TIME _____ AM/PM

M _____

OF _____

PHONE (_____) _____

Telephoned		Please call	
Will call back		Returned call	
Came by		Wants to meet	

Message _____

_____

_____

_____

Signed _____

FILL IN THE TELEPHONE MESSAGE ABOVE: ↑

Urgent	=	✔
To	=	Elizabeth
Date	=	Today's date
Time	=	9:00 AM
M	=	Ms. Jones
Of	=	The pharmacy
Phone	=	(202) 977–0000
Telephoned	=	✔
Message	=	Your medicine is ready.
Signed	=	Your name

MONEY ORDER

EXAMPLE: $75.25

```
┌─────────────────────────────────────────────────────────────┬──────────────┐
│         ABC–XYZ MONEY ORDER COMPANY          ⇦                │              │
│                                                               │              │
│                              MONEY ORDER                      │              │
│ PAY TO THE                                                    │   $75.25     │
│ ORDER OF ___ Friend's name ___  ★ ★ ★ ★ $75.25               │              │
│        PURCHASER AGREES TO SERVICE CHARGE                     │              │
│   Your signature here          75 DOLLARS★★★★★★               │              │
│        PURCHASER SIGNATURE      25 CENTS★★★★★★★                │              │
│                                                               │              │
│         Your address here                                     │              │
│              ADDRESS                                          │ K H 0378547  │
│                                                               │              │
│ K H 0378547   1119100000000:118  03700000000                 │    ⇦         │
└─────────────────────────────────────────────────────────────┴──────────────┘
```

FILL OUT THE MONEY ORDER:

Pay to   =   Your friend
Purchaser   =   You
Address   =   Your address
Amount   = $75.25

```
┌─────────────────────────────────────────────────────────────┬──────────────┐
│         ABC–XYZ MONEY ORDER COMPANY          ⇦                │              │
│                                                               │              │
│                              MONEY ORDER                      │              │
│ PAY TO THE                                                    │   $75.25     │
│ ORDER OF _____  ★ ★ ★ ★ $75.25                 │              │
│        PURCHASER AGREES TO SERVICE CHARGE                     │              │
│   _____          75 DOLLARS★★★★★★               │              │
│        PURCHASER SIGNER          25 CENTS★★★★★★★               │              │
│                                                               │              │
│   _____                                         │              │
│              ADDRESS                                          │ K H 0378547  │
│                                                               │              │
│ K H 0378547   1119100000000:118  03700000000                 │    ⇦         │
└─────────────────────────────────────────────────────────────┴──────────────┘
```

MONEY ORDER

FILL OUT THE MONEY ORDER

Amount = $50.00

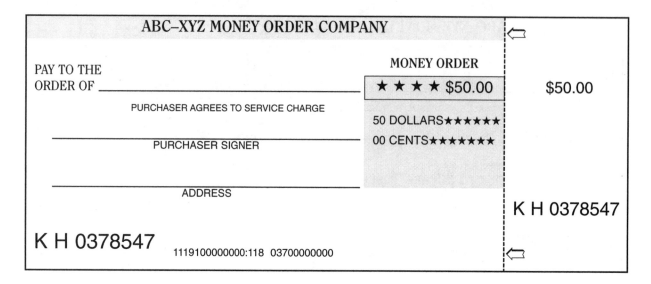

FILL OUT THE MONEY ORDER

Amount = $67.50

ABC–XYZ MONEY ORDER COMPANY

PAY TO THE
ORDER OF _____

MONEY ORDER

★ ★ ★ ★ $67.50

$67.50

PURCHASER AGREES TO SERVICE CHARGE

67 DOLLARS★★★★★★

_____

50 CENTS★★★★★★★

PURCHASER SIGNER

_____

ADDRESS

K H 0378547

K H 0378547
1119100000000:118 03700000000

PRACTICE WRITING

PRACTICE WRITING

PRACTICE WRITING

PRACTICE WRITING

PRACTICE WRITING

PRACTICE WRITING

PRACTICE WRITING

PRACTICE WRITING

PRACTICE WRITING

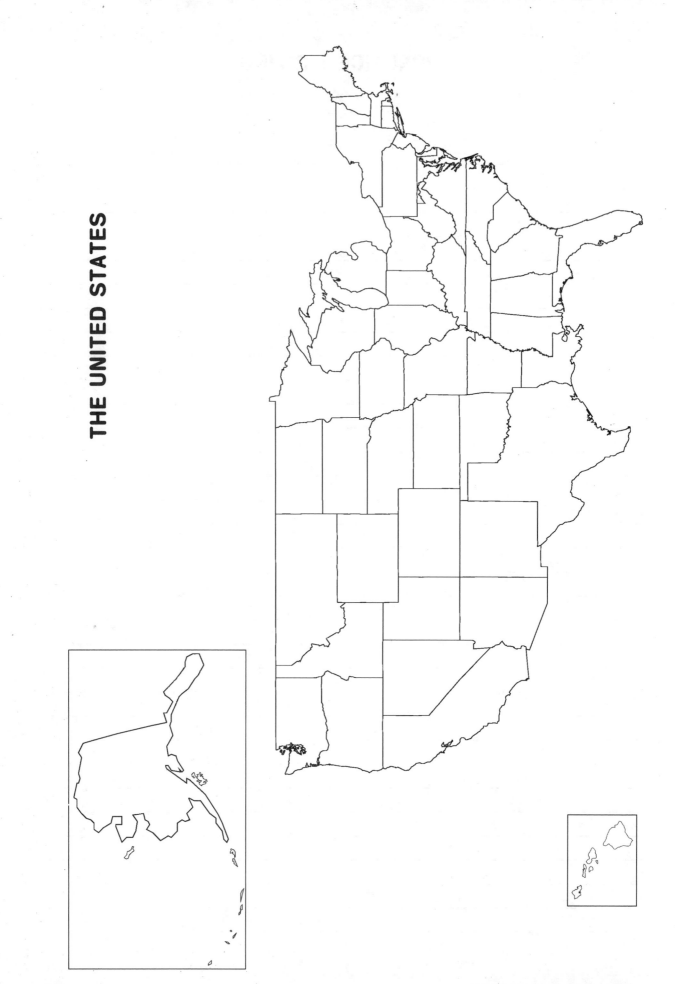

THE UNITED STATES

American Handwriting